How to Gossip Nicely:

A Southerner Ponders the Grapevine

SUSAN TAYLOR BLOCK

Susan Taylor Block

Betty Baird Rusher

Featuring Illustrations by A. B. Moore
and Recipes by Betty Baird Rusher

ISBN: 1-4392-4903-2
EAN13: 9781439249031

Visit www.booksurge.com to order additional copies.

Robert Hill Camp, Copy Editor

Table of Contents

Disclaimer

This handbook is meant as a guide for those who delight in staying abreast of the who, what, where, when, why, and how of community life. Being part of a "good gossip" network is fun and healthy. However, "bad gossip," venomous communication that is designed to control, hurt, or destroy, is strongly discouraged.

How to Gossip Nicely

Mean Versus Nice

Grapevines with their tendrils, twisted branches, and corkscrew trunks have long been associated with gossip -- casually transmitted news that travels a meandering path. Grapevines can yield delectable pleasure in the form of sun-warmed fruit, but they're also known to be favorite haunts for snakes. Figuring out which news to transmit, and which to put away mentally in the "Remember this, but keep it quiet" file marks the difference between being a malicious gossip or simply staying connected to the community.

Acceptable gossip covers quite a number of topics. Major life events such as births, weddings, and graduations are standard forms of good gossip. So are the myriad reports of who's moving, newly employed, laid off, splitting up, the "dating report," new purchases, the latest party, or the cute new shop around the corner. Slightly more sensational topics include reports of Nancy's diving neckline and soaring hemline, or aging Mike's new buff physique and red convertible. Reports of flamboyant behavior are fun, too, and can spark up a dry news day.

Malicious gossip is, however, news that hurts. It hurts the subject, the messenger, and the listener. News of seriously bad behavior, surprises concerning paternity, criminal acts, or atrocities may or may not be true, particularly if a divorce or money squabble is involved. The most sinister gossipers know how to fold a bit of truth into the batter, making the lies seem more credible.

Even if news of a bad sort is true, it doesn't help to pass it along. Though it is nice to be "in the know," people who actually delight in the sins of others are pretty hard-up for fun. After all, dwelling on the faults or defeats of others is depressing and has a tendency to drag the news bearer down. Pointing one finger makes three more point back at the toxic gossiper.

It is less painful to be gossiped about than to recognize oneself as a hurtful gossiper. Years ago, a girlfriend shared an embarrassing secret with me. It made me sad to hear it, but at the same time I felt such an urge to share the news. Finally, I divulged the secret to another friend with the customary stipulation, "Please don't tell this to anyone else."

Of course, the news got out. That multiplied my girlfriend's embarrassment and made me feel awful. I'm sure I shared other things that I shouldn't have before I made a serious effort to try and change my ways.

Over time, I have found happiness on those occasions that I refused to transmit toxic gossip and altered the focus in order to say something nice about the person being verbally charred. Saying something positive actually felt like blowing kisses. I hoped that this might create a little breeze that would fan out and eventually refresh that person's world.

It's important to use common sense when filtering out poison gossip. While it is a good thing to stop a chain of toxic gossip near to its source, unless you find the news is untrue, don't forget what you've heard. It could keep you from trusting your retirement account to an embezzler -- or finding yourself on a date with your half-brother or sister!

Even by excluding pernicious gossip from the choices available to the average "Chatty Cathy," plenty of fun can still be had by staying alert and keeping abreast of events around us. After all, it is only natural to want to know about things in which friends, neighbors, relatives, political candidates, and even a celebrity or two are involved. A reformed gossip can still stay connected, thus keeping up what is going on around them -- the good, the funny, the eccentric, and the unexpected. To slam the door on all news would be like living in isolation -- a sentence reserved for very few.

Special Equipment
for the Good Gossiper

Cell phones

While there are many ways to transmit news, cell phones may be the best for they are with us at all times. Their ring tones light up the screen and our faces with the possibility of interesting happenings. Catching up on current events redeems what would simply have been a boring moment or a long wait somewhere.

Remember that the cloak of darkness can add a negative edge to news exchanges. If you are overly tired or have imbibed any alcohol whatsoever, do not engage in nocturnal gossip. It will reduce your resolve to avoid toxic gossip and could even lead to autobiographical revelations - a case in which the gossiper could instantly become the victim.

Beware of those tiny little buttons that are capable of automatic callback or that dial straight from your phone's directory of numbers. If you accidently touch, mash, or sit on your phone the wrong way, you might learn later that your personal conversation was overheard via the airwaves by a friend on the other end. This friend has, in turn, broadcasted the details to others. Beware of falling asleep with your phone in your bed for if you roll over on it during the night the wrong way, there's no telling *what* you might be sharing.

Knife and Fork

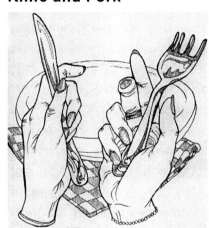

"Doing lunch" is more complex than a telephone conversation because there is so much more for the senses to take in. At lunch in a diner, cafe, or restaurant, your eyes are busy examining your surroundings -- and the accompanying people. There are napkins, tablecloths, bare gleaming surfaces, glasses of all sorts, china, flowers, menus and dining chairs. Then there are the sounds of a restaurant - the clink, clack, clanging that goes on continually whether there is music to mask it or not.

Then there's also the cursory allowed sweep to see who else is in the restaurant, and, maybe, who is not. Just in terms of clothing alone, a busy restaurant is a fleeting quilt of many colors and textures. You may also be fretting about whether you should eat crepes or salad, chocolate or fruit; and trying not to eat gluttonously -- or to stare at the backside of the good looking, beautifully built male server when he walks away from the table.

Nevertheless, lunch is usually enjoyable and allows just enough time to give and receive the newest news at surface level. If you wish a longer span of time to get more details with your news, join a luncheon bridge club. Bridge itself is civilized hand-to-hand combat, but extended periods of play come with their own landmines. If there's a spat, sloppy play, or a cell phone conversation lasting longer than 30 seconds, that will become tomorrow's grapevine news. Above all, never say the words, "Now, what was trumps?"

Athletic Shoes

Exercise of any sort provides fellowship, but activities that involve lots of walking are best for communication. Whether walking down the golf course or on a regular sidewalk route with neighborhood friends, "The Walk" gives you time to catch up on everything. Topics can range from one girlfriend's long distance romance to another's humorous struggles as a kindergarten teacher. Naturally, there are moments when everyone falls silent during a walk, but

that just creates a space in which you can remember what it was you forgot to tell.

Over time, members of "Walkie-Talkie" groups learn which topics are looked upon as taboo. A short list might include anything too risqué for the most ladylike among you, bragging about college basketball scores if there are fanatics among you who root for rivals, or vivid descriptions of chocolate desserts if there is even one dieter in the bunch. Religion and politics, per all our parental advice of long ago, are also delicate subjects.

No matter what the topic, the most important thing is to keep to the Walkers' Motto. With apologies to the Las Vegas trademark, "What's said on the walk stays on the walk." Of course, that is an impossible goal to achieve, but serious effort to that end earns points.

The Car

Like the settings for phone conversations and walking group chatter, there's something about not facing each other "in the car" that promotes revelation. This can work in many types of relationships in which news is shared, but is particularly effective with young teenagers. Tooling along down a scenic highway creates a mood that can actually move them to share some little bit of news with their mothers. Never share their secrets.

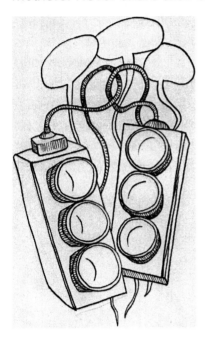

Even in-town driving with all its stoplight and tie-up delays can be a boost for sharing. Just being safely enclosed with someone amidst the roar and ruckus of surrounding traffic can create a feeling of intimacy that can prevail without even a glance at one another. The day a teenager gets a driver's license is not only a scary one for the mother, but often a sad one because time spent "in the car" together becomes scarce.

Electronic Mail

Electronic mail transmissions, of course known as e-mail in today's text message jargon, should be used primarily to set up dates to meet friends. It should be avoided as an avenue of news communication because emails can be forwarded instantaneously, both accidently and intentionally. News that interests one person might antagonize another. Avoid even those inverted character summaries, such as the statement, "Victoria was sober Tuesday night."

If you are still tempted to email gossip, picture one of those little planes that flies above a crowded beach displaying a long advertising banner. Now, visualize <u>your email</u> fluttering down the beach behind that plane. The difference would be that the last words on the banner would be your name and email address.

Forms of Gossip

Routine Announcements

Routine announcements are the most harmless form of casual communication, as in, "I hear Daphne got an engagement ring Saturday night." Happy occasions and meritorious achievements fall in this category, as well as more mundane news such as relating the score of a game of golf or a tennis match. Unfortunately, sad news is a part of life, too, and critical illness, death, and burial fall into this category as well.

The list of routine announcement possibilities also includes, but is not limited to: births, christenings, bar and bat mizvahs, college acceptance, graduations, marriages, promotions, awards, changes of residence, notable vacations, and significant events in the lives of people's pets.

"Gossip Game" Blunders

Just like the old game in which a whispered statement is accidentally morphed as it's passed around a room full of people, sometimes real news is misspoken and misheard. "Daphne got a ring," becomes "Def'nitely gonna' rain." In the same manner, "The Deacon did no heavy tipping," becomes "The deaconess went skinny dipping."

In the real world, sometimes the message is mangled in someone's mind rather than over the air waves. If you encounter someone who tends to get names and facts confused, limit your conversations with them to weather and gardening tips. If you discover someone is using real names and events, but mixing things up intentionally, regard them as you would a billboard.

News Concerning Eccentrics

News of eccentrics and their whimsical ways might be the most refreshing form of all gossip. Those who are fortunate enough to have eccentrics in their midst will have a storehouse of things to talk about for years to come. Eccentrics are usually harmless and many are downright lovable. They tend to flourish in art communities, Great Britain, and throughout the American South.

Eccentrics cover a wide range of habits and traits. They often have colorful personalities and unique lifestyles. If Daphne were an eccentric, then the news might be told thusly: "Daphne's getting married. She finally found her match. She wears nothing but blue and he wears nothing but red and white. Oh, and they're getting married on the Fourth of July!"

Living in the South, I have met some delightful eccentrics. I knew a retired businessman who once had a small donkey for a pet. He took the donkey on rides around town and the big-eared animal sat in the passenger seat like a person. One day, he took the donkey into a small grocery store. When the owner erupted, my friend said, "But the sign says, 'No Dogs.'" On another occasion, he took the donkey to a cocktail party. "Well, what do you know?" said the hostess after the party was in full swing, "I think your donkey is the best behaved ass at this party."

My home town alone has produced many other fine eccentrics. A financially comfortable, otherwise sedentary woman would walk 10 blocks to the power company office to pay her bill rather than sacrificing the cost of a postage stamp. One of our county's largest landowners was occasionally mistaken for a needy person because he still farmed by choice and tended to show up in holey clothes, trailing corn silks and soil. I've heard that he toted so many ripe crops as gifts to friends that vegetables began to grow from seed in the crevices of his car.

One easy-going lady took a piece of mail across the street to her neighbor's house, about 1990. "This was delivered to my house by mistake," she said when she handed it to them. After she returned home, they noticed the postmark. The letter had been sitting on her famously cluttered desk for almost twenty years before she got around to rerouting it.

Our local eccentrics run the gamut. They have been known to bury cash in jars and hide diamonds in the sock drawer. One esteemed attorney and Episcopal vestryman used to call for lengthy sermons to end by tapping his cane loudly on the old church floor. A senior Southern belle displayed the body of her newly departed husband wearing full military garb in the midst of a scheduled historic mansion tour, thus giving tourists a clearer picture of old Southern customs than they anticipated. If not for space issues, I could go on and on.

True eccentrics just are. It is as difficult for an unconventional person to disappear into the crowd as it would be for a conformist to feign peculiarity. There is much to celebrate in the natural manifestations of eccentricity.

Announcements With Commentary

Commentary can slant to many different angles depending on the nature and life experiences of the teller. "I'm glad Daphne's finally engaged, because she's been trying to snare somebody for almost thirty years," is what one disgruntled gossip might say. Another take could be, "Daphne's been too darn selective." If stated in a catty and clever enough fashion, such comments can linger for years.

Exaggerated News

Exaggeration is generally used to make someone look worse than they are. It's not only mean, but milks degree out of discernment. It takes mental effort, not meanness, to peg a person accurately with words. So the lazy, axe-grinding gossip might say, "I hear Daphne's getting married and her fiancé is the homeliest man on earth."

Almost everyone exaggerates occasionally, but serial exaggerators risk losing their audience — a fate worse than their cell phone tower toppling over during a steel makers' strike. The news bearer should think before she speaks. Saying, " Daphne's getting married and I hear her fiancé has never been mistaken for Brad Pitt," would at least be an improvement.

Sometimes news exaggeration is just a figment of curmudgeonation. Identify the bad-tempered among you and take what they say with a grain of pepper. Some of these people, as the old saying goes, "just can't he'p it."

Bad Penny News

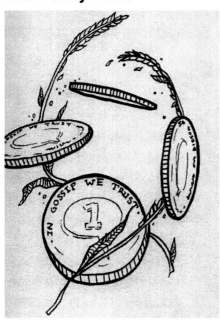

Like that bad old penny, this type of gossip keeps coming back — over and over. If Daphne wet her pants right in the middle of the first grade stage play, someone will remember it and repeat it when her name enters the gossip circle again. "Daphne's engaged! Remember when the teacher closed the curtain so she could wade across the stage? Ha, ha, ha!"

When a malicious gossiper sets out to "dig up dirt" on someone, they are likely to find a few pennies in the soil. It's sad that some people truly delight in the shortcomings of others, but especially so when one or more of the pennies is a counterfeit and old lies begin circulating all over again.

Celebrity Gossip

Celebrity Gossip is a category of news telling best left to the media and teenagers. Celebrities today tend to be young and their tenures of fame short. Adults often mangle their names and juxtapose them with other national newsmakers. The results bring sighs from their teenage children that could sail a paper boat across a fish pond.

Using past knowledge as a defense doesn't help. Your teenager doesn't care if you once knew a page full of biographical facts about each Beatle or wrote a term paper analyzing the autobiographical aspects of lyrics by Mick Jagger. Just give up before you embarrass yourself further.

"Daphne's engaged," said the mother to her teenage daughter. "He looks like Justice Timberline, but he's a real he-man."

"It's Justin Timberlake, Mom, and I believe he is metrosexual."

"So, he only likes to have sex in cities?"

"(Sigh)"

News With Negative Ascribed Motives

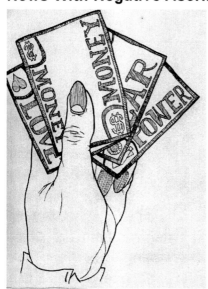

"I hear Daphne got engaged Saturday night, but I think she's just marrying him for his fine new car." Like a daytime soap opera characterization, there is little gray in the world of ascribed motives. To a self righteous or bitter person, it's not enough to merely report the news. It must be analyzed in such a way that the subject is lowered a rung or two. This is where the grapevine begins to turn into a snakevine. Beware of guessing motivation. It's tricky and sometimes reveals more about the talebearer than the tale's subject. The complexities of it are best left to those too wise to talk about it.

Prevarications

Fabricated news is a wholly unacceptable form of gossip. It is like turning a corkscrew in someone's back. Those who do this usually fall into one of two categories:

criminals or women who are jealous. For instance, Daphne's new mother-in-law is so jealous of Daphne that she invents a damaging story about her and chooses to spread it, of all places, at the couple's wedding reception. This is an actual example of prevarication gossip that occurred in my hometown.

"Did you know the bride seduced my son back when his first wife was dying of cancer?" asked the mother-in-law to a variety of guests in the ballroom.

"Then, she had the audacity to go to the funeral. Later that afternoon, she came to my front door and announced, 'Your son is mine now!'"

The full motivation for such lies is a mystery, but it's a sure fact that they loiter in the minds of certain hearers for years and are sometimes retold with gusto and embellishment. The person who invents a lie to hurt someone else is a shadow version of an assassin.

A subcategory to lying is termite planting. This is when a gnawing hint of destructive misinformation is embedded in the hearer's memory. Sometimes even truth can turn into a termite if twisted the wrong way. Planting termites of either variety requires perfect timing and the wiles of a fox. Unless you are a courtroom attorney, if you are clever enough to do this well, you should be using your considerable talent for something more noble.

ABC's of Troubleshooting

Absenting oneself too early – Never be the first one to leave a gathering of gossips. Stay until the hen party's over, or you might be the one left frying in the skillet. And, if the gathering happens to be part of a family reunion, bolt yourself to your seat. Relatives have a way of grafting grapevines and family trees so that virtually every member of the family risks being hung out on a limb.

Bridge party ruckus - This is most often the result of someone from one table overhearing what she is not supposed to hear from the offending table. This can be largely avoided by practicing "indoors-at-church voices."

Cousinhood calamity – *Never* share even the blandest scuttlebutt with anyone if it concerns members of their

own family. If they have already heard it, they will shame you by letting you know they did. "Of *course* I know that - our grandmothers were sisters," they might say. In the South, even if the connection is more distant, they're liable to take offense. That's the place where embroidered family trees serve as cherished wall hangings, and the term "first cousins, once removed," is still understood as a diagrammed genealogical relationship rather than a marriage that was annulled hastily because of too much kindred blood.

If you continue to offend, visit the local genealogical library and learn who is related. Whether surnames match, or not, isn't important because Mrs. Michael Powers could be sister to Mrs. Warren Andrews, who, as you just reported to Ms. Powers, "dared sachet out on the Magnolia Club tennis court in an outfit that was of fine quality, but much too revealing."

Most of all, remember the words of a Bishop's wife who moved to her husband's Southern hometown. "If you have anything bad to say about anyone here, go into a closet and talk to yourself because most of these people are related."

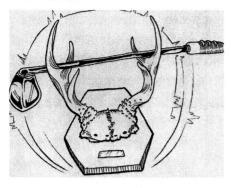

Duck and cover – If *ever* you hear that anybody's husband shot any living animal "out of season," do not pass it on. Men who are nice and smart otherwise become cavemen in camouflage when they sit in deer stands and bird blinds all day. Don't try to kid your way out of it either. Husbands have no sense of humor about hunting: ditto golf.

Evidence to the contrary - When confronted with facts that negate your story, immediately apologize and mentally mark the teller off your list of trusted informers. Then, change the subject quickly and talk steadily so there is no room for interruption. Suggested lead-in topics include a travel story, or some honor a young relative has just earned in school.

Fur - Avoid all gossip having to do with the subject of fur lest it fly in your face. Fake fur is an offense to fur coat enthusiasts and snobs. Real fur angers animal rights activists and sends a mixed message to house pets. So even if you can distinguish a fake fur from a real one at forty paces, it is best to keep your own trap shut.

Ginger Snap – Passive-aggressive folks can stay calm and gingerly sweet when you tell them something, then snap back at you with a whip a few days later. "You *know* I used the same decorator you said uses too much red," they might say with their face matching the color. When dealing with Ginger Snaps, it's best to let them do the talking.

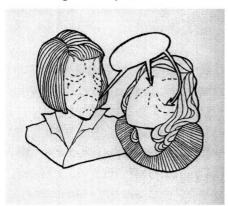

Having work done – News of friends undergoing optional plastic surgery should be avoided, especially in face-to-face gossip sessions. Just the mention of it causes the hearer to examine your own face, or you figure, more carefully. "Well, isn't it about time you did the same thing?" they might be thinking. On the other hand, if you happen to be fortunate enough to have natural good looks, they will be studying you and pondering just what you have done in the way of work and which doctor you used.

In hot water – Hot tubs tend to melt inhibitions and fry jealous tempers. Never tell what you saw there, or what you didn't see. Better yet, get a membership to an unheated Y pool.

Just one person - A wise man said, "Two people can keep a secret if one of them is dead." Never trust anyone with a big secret unless they have proven, over time, to keep the little ones quiet.

Kiddie sports melee - All you said was, "I think that umpire needs glasses," and the next thing you knew, you felt like a bleacher pillow under a sumo wrestler. Whether Little League Baseball or Junior Lacrosse, keep quiet as a stadium mouse who's watching that piece of popcorn you just dropped.

Leaf blower stopped - You've been shouting to be heard above a neighbor's leaf blower, so when the noise stops abruptly, everyone at your picnic, including Shelly, hears you say to the person next to you, "Looks like lightning struck Shelly's hair today." You're busted. If applicable, mollify the poor girl by talking about your last home permanent and how you "just wish" you had more body in your hair.

Mobile misplacement - If you've lost your digital friend, buy another cell phone immediately. You never know what great stories you might have missed while looking for the old one. If your budget is stretched too much to buy a new phone, use a "treat" reward system to train your dog to find cell phones. If that works, train him to find your remote control, too. They should all come with leashes.

Naked as a Jaybird - Happening upon a portly but distinguished neighbor lying naked in a secluded patio hammock can be a shocker. Tiptoe away, blame it on hot weather, and go home and pour yourself some lemonade to cool your tongue. Jaybird stories are best kept to yourself, but you will probably tell *some*one.

Office cubicle blunder – Just because an office mate is out of sight doesn't mean they can't hear you through that thin mesh partition.

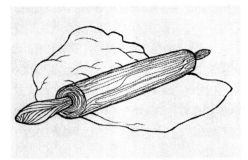

Pie in your face – Suppose you have a friend who is known to be an excellent cook and you're sure she leaves some ingredient out of each recipe she shares so she can remain the local cooking queen. Don't try to discover the secret ingredient. If you do, don't share it with others or your friend might soon let you know what it feels like to be pie dough under a rolling pin. And if the ingredient happens to be a bit of store-bought cake mix, you will immediately know what it is like to be a piece of steak under a meat-tenderizing mallet.

Queen of Hearts glare - If you choose to spread good news or compliments, you always take the risk of having been kind to someone on the Queen of Hearts' Hit List. Like the Walt Disney rendering of the Queens of Hearts from <u>Alice in Wonderland</u>, these women glare, declare, and make heads roll. They like to have the upper hand in determining the "A" and "B" lists and don't like it when the "balance" is upset. Pity the person who floats to the top of the barrel, for control may await her in the form of a croquet mallet. If by your words or by your being you've enraged a

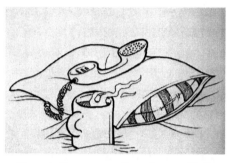

Queen of Hearts, curtsy, bite your tongue, and go your merry way.

Red-eye special – Some women prefer sharing news by phone very late at night. It's like pillow talk, but without the complications. If the news is interesting, rally to stay awake, but just listen. If it happens often, either turn off the phone or cultivate the art of napping.

Sunday Potshots – Unless it's in the form of information only, church gossip is simply too easy to be allowed. There's no sport to it. There we are for an hour looking at the backs of heads we know so well. It's so easy for the one who eats too much to talk about the one who drinks too much; for the chief name-dropper to criticize the affected self-proclaimed societal expert; and for the covetous ones to take aim at the smug ones. Most folks who attend church are at least trying, so everyone there deserves a reprieve.

Travel blackout - Travel can seriously hamper your ability to stay in-the know. High roaming fees, visits to Internet challenged areas, and being elbow-to-elbow with anti-gossiping spouses are situations that mimic hedge clippers in a grapevine. Plan short trips and schedule lunch with your best friends the day after you return home.

Unusually bad housekeeping - If a house is semi-dusty and strewn throughout with stacks of fine reading material, you may describe the owner as interesting and somewhat eccentric. If a dwelling is strewn with all nature of things, say nothing. Note: If it's a multi-generational beach house and it appears neat, something is wrong, too. Ferret it out.

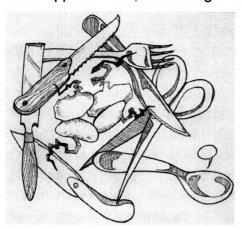

Vicious Circle - If you notice that your best girlfriends are all talking trash about each other in their absence, find another circle. It's OK to speak about friends with affection, realism, and humor in their absence, but if there are any chisels in sight, break away permanently. They will talk about you worse when you're gone, but at least you won't be influenced by them anymore.

Wedded Un-bliss - It's OK to pass along news of a separation or divorce, but refrain from saying much else. An outsider's interpretation of a marriage or a divorce is about as valuable as thrown rice. Unless you've witnessed the upbringing of both parties, can read their minds, and are present in the bedroom with them, you cannot know the reason people choose who they choose, or leave whom they leave. The complexities of attraction and compatibility are beyond sidewalk analysis. Sometimes the mistake is in the breaking up, but sometimes it was in the marrying.

X-Ray talk – Bad health news doesn't need to be repeated unless it's done behind closed doors, and shared with family members or those whose lives are "closely linked" with the patient's. If you are pressed unmercifully to violate this rule, just say, "Maybe she broke her finger?"

You're on the phone too much – Make the best use of your telephone time. Play background music that makes you want to dance, then don fuzzy socks. Use the socks to dust mop floors and wipe down moldings and chair railings - all to the rhythm of the songs. To get your heart rate up and keep it there long enough to do any good, walk fast through or around your house at least 50 times.

Zirconium - Just because it looks big doesn't mean it's fake. Purse your lips, please.

Backyard Muscadine Grapevines

If you're fortunate enough to live in the American South, there's a possibility that you can grow delectable muscadine grapes in your own backyard. As early as 1701, English explorer John Lawson "discovered" a bronze-colored variety of grapes Native Americans had been eating and preserving for centuries. They were scuppernongs, a cultivar of muscadine grapes that are known formally as Vitis rotundifolia or Muscadiniana rotundifolia. Bullis grapes, another old form of muscadines, are nearly black in color. Dr. Barclay Poling and Connie Fisk of the North Carolina State University Horticultural Science Department also recommend these new muscadine varieties: Carlos, Doreen, Nobel, Magnolia, and Nesbitt.

In addition to having their own natural defenses against many pest and maladies, muscadine grapes provide a blast of antioxidants to the ingester. A backyard grapevine can be viewed as nature's elixir and, for centuries, children of all ages have been spotted under them, eating and spewing. The seeds must go and the hulls are tough, but the juice of sun-warmed muscadines tastes like something straight from the Garden of Eden.

Grapevines grow best in sunny spots that have good soil and drainage. Too much shade and almost any puddling will destroy the plant. Vines should be planted 10' to 20' apart in spring after there is any risk of a freeze. Trellises for each vine should measure at least 10' by 6', and should be installed before planting. Vines must be trained, pruned, and fertilized -- a manageable task for the backyard gardener. Consult online resources for more information on grapevine cultivation, and the benefits and warnings concerning grapes and grape products.

Recipes from the Grapevine

by Betty Baird Rusher

Betty Baird Rusher is one of my walking buddies and the best cook I know. Several of us "girls" wander through our neighborhood or the mall here in Wilmington, NC, almost every day. Walking breeds chatter, and after I began rattling on about grapevines, Betty started cooking up scrumptious grape dishes. The taste tests were a writer's gravy.

A few of these recipes call for muscadine grape products or wine. The products in capsule form are readily available in health food stores and online. Some of the best muscadine juice and wine in the country is produced in Duplin County, North Carolina.

The muscadine dishes are favorites of mine and bring back a variety of memories. When I was a little girl, scuppernong vines were common backyard sights in my neighborhood. After some older boys raided my grandmother's grapevine one afternoon, a girlfriend and I donned homemade cross belts and toted cap guns and rubber daggers in a weak effort to guard the grapevine from more thievery. That's how much we *loved* those grapes!

Seedless Grape Appetizer
Here, the grapes add texture more than taste.

4 ounces cream cheese
2 tablespoons crushed pineapple with juice
1 tablespoon Deviled Smithfield Ham Spread
12 drops Tabasco Sauce (or more, to taste)
1 teaspoon sugar
1 cup sliced seedless red or green grapes
Almond slices, toasted

To soften cream cheese, add pineapple, ham, Tabasco, and sugar. When well blended fold in grapes, place in serving bowl, and sprinkle with toasted almonds. Serve with your favorite crackers or chips.

Frozen Grape Salad
Substitute other fresh fruits such as peaches to keep this dish from becoming too predictable. Poppy seeds add eye appeal.

1 1/2 cups green or red seedless grapes, halved.
1 small sliced banana
1 small can crushed pineapple
1/4 cup chopped nuts (pecans, walnuts, or your own choice)
3 tablespoons brown sugar

1 tablespoon lemon juice
1/2 pint sour cream
1/2 teaspoon poppy seeds (optional)

Mix grapes, pineapples, banana, nuts, brown sugar, sour cream and poppy seeds. Spread in 8 x 8 pan and freeze. Cut in squares and serve on lettuce leaf or pour into individual salad molds. Top with sprig of mint or a dollop of sour cream.

Fresh Grape Salad with Ginger Dressing
This salad is also good with other seasonal fruits.

1 cup seedless halved green or red grapes
1 cup fresh pineapple cut in small chunks
1 cup sliced strawberries

Mix fruits and place servings in lettuce "cups." Top with Ginger Dressing.

Ginger Dressing
Stem ginger is found in food specialty shops.

1 8 ounce package softened cream cheese
4 pieces of finely chopped stem ginger.
1 tablespoon syrup from stem ginger
1/4 cup orange juice or crushed pineapple with juice
1 scant teaspoon of sugar

Mix cream cheese, chopped ginger, ginger syrup, orange juice and sugar. If thinner dressing is desired, add more orange juice.

Chicken with Muscadine Sauce and Red Grapes
This is a hearty winter dish.

1 tablespoon butter
1 teaspoon minced garlic
1 cup muscadine wine
1 cup chicken broth
1 tablespoon orange juice concentrate
1 tablespoon soy sauce
1 tablespoon tomato paste
1/4 teaspoon red pepper flakes
1/2 teaspoon salt
1/4 teaspoon black pepper
1 1/2 cup sliced red seedless grapes
4 chicken breasts of 6 smaller pieces of chicken
Butter for sautéing

In saucepan, melt tablespoon of butter and sauté garlic. Add muscadine wine, chicken broth, orange juice concentrate, soy sauce, tomato paste, red pepper flakes, salt and pepper. Stir and simmer while preparing chicken.

Roll chicken pieces in flour, salt, and pepper, then sauté in butter. When chicken is brown, pour muscadine sauce over chicken and add grapes.

If pan used to brown chicken can be used in oven, cover and place in 350 degree oven 45 minutes to one hour - or until chicken is practically falling off the bones. If pan is not ovenproof, place in oven proof dish with sauce, and cover with foil. Cook to specifications above. Serve chicken and sauce over rice.

Scuppernong Cream
This is a very smooth and rich dessert.

2 packages Knox gelatin
1/3 cup milk
2 cups half and half
2 tablespoons scuppernong wine
2 tablespoons XXX confectionary sugar
Zest of one orange

Dissolve Knox gelatin in 1/3 cup milk. In a saucepan, place half and half, 3 tablespoons of scuppernong wine, 3 tablespoons confectionary sugar, and zest of one orange. Bring to a simmer, remove from heat, add dissolved gelatin and stir well.

Let gelatine mixture cool at room temperature for one hour. When mixture has cooled, fold in 1/2 pint whipping cream that has been whipped very stiff with one tablespoon confectionary sugar. Pour in individual molds and refrigerate.

In saucepan place 3/4 cup scuppernong wine, 1/4 cup orange juice, and 2 tablespoons sugar. Let simmer until reduced by half. Refrigerate. Serve the unmolded scuppernong cream on dessert plates. Drizzle with a little of the scuppernong orange syrup and garnish with mint leaf. Serve with a small cookie or wafer.

Spring Fizzie
Whether this drink is the fountain of youth - or not, it's refreshing and strangely filling.

1 capsule grape hull and seed powdered extract (contents only)
Grape Juice
Frozen seedless grapes
Sparkling water

Add the contents of one grape extract capsule to a glass of pure grape juice, and stir well. Add frozen grapes to cool and enjoy. A dash of sparkling water provides the fizz. If more sweetness is desired, add a dash of Simply Syrup (see blelow.) Garnish with a slice of lemon and mint leaf. This drink will be good to the last munched grape.

Simply Syrup
Mint is the secret.

1 cup sugar
1 cup water
2 or 3 sprigs of fresh mint
Place sugar, water, and mint in a saucepan and bring to a boil. Stir unti sugar dissolves. Strain, refrigerate, and us as needed in summer drink.

Acknowledgments

I am proud to be artist A. B. Moore's great-aunt and delighted with the work she contributed to this book. Betty Baird Rusher is a legendary local cook and her recipes add much to this slender volume. In addition to being copy editor, Robert Hill Camp has been a consultant throughout the writing process.

The following people told no gossip but did provide me with a lot of happy camaraderie while this book was being written: Betty Rusher, Jeff Newell, Robert Camp, Jessie Leigh Boney, Bob Lane, Bob Warren, Lillian Boney, Jean Graham, Dotty Weathersbee, Cecilia Budd Grimes, Taylor Cromartie, Catherine Gerdes, Jay Taylor, Brenda Manus, Peggy Perdew, John Symmes, Nancy Symmes, Elaine Henson, John C. Drewry, and Tookie Keffer.

The Team

Author Susan Taylor Block is a native of Wilmington, NC where she grew up in the midst of small camellia gardens, grapevines, and pineapple sand pear trees. One day a pygmy rattler slithered through the side door of her house and she hoed him to death on the hardwood floor.

Artist A. B. Moore was born in Charleston, SC, and raised in Charlotte, NC. She is a 2009 graduate of Northwest School of the Arts and one of the nation's important emerging artists. She is currently pursuing undergraduate work at the Maryland Institute College of Art.

Recipe contributor Betty Baird Rusher grew up in Oxford, NC. Her grandmother welcomed her childhood cooking efforts and always gave her her own piece of dough and a chopping block. She never had to clean up or wash dishes and was always allowed to serve the mint and cheese straws at her grandmother's Saturday Afternoon Book Club.

Robert H. Camp is a something of a Renaissance Man, and Virginia Gentleman. Primarily and personally, he is a devoted father and husband who loves all things outdoors, including hunting, fishing and boating. Professionally, he is an English professor, writing instructor, and editor.

Made in the USA